I0178057

ISBN-13: 978-1-7338173-9-4

Dedication

To any teacher who has left work at the end of the day questioning the decision you made to become a teacher...

This book is for you

GUERRILLA WARFARE TEACHING MANEUVERS

INTRODUCTION

Fight Like a Guerrilla

GUERRILLA WARFARE IS A BATTLE between unequal forces. The primary goal of the Guerrilla solider is not only to defeat the adversary but to win support and influence while doing it. Guerrilla **maneuvers** magnify the impact of a small, mobile force against the larger enemy camp. If successful, guerrillas weaken their opposition with calculated procedural advances, forcing them to withdraw and comply. Tactically, guerrillas tend to avoid open confrontation with rebel troops, preferring to attack covertly; depleting the opposing force and minimizing their own losses. Guerrilla warriors optimize the elements of mobility, and surprise, taking full advantage of their terrain. For more information about thIs read The Art of War by Sun Tzu.

Friend, if you've ever been in an out-of-control classroom, you're in the enemy's camp. Consider yourself in the trenches of Guerrilla Warfare. Know that you are outnumbered and must initiate precise tactical measures to recover territory and govern the learning environment.

Imagine you're a guest walking into a classroom of 32 students. As soon as you enter, you are bombarded with chatter, noises, and giggling. Three kids are out of their seat, others are checking their phones or watching YouTube videos. You notice one girl in the back braiding another's hair, while two boys shoot rubber bands at each other. Making your way up to the teacher, you step on Cheetos and candy wrappers. There's a sign that says "No Eating in Class" posted above the whiteboard. The teacher begins to deliver a lesson to five pupils in front who appear to be listening. Upon your approach, the teacher turns and stares curiously at you, as if to say you might be interrupting something. As a guest, what would your first impression be?

If you've just shrugged in disbelief thinking, "Wow, I don't have it that bad" — just wait. Allowing any level of disruption or off task behavior, without a swift and decisive correction, will inevitably lead to chaos. As a veteran teacher, I can bear witness. Many intelligent and compassionate educators have at some point fallen victim to an out-of-control class and felt powerless to do much about it. I'm in a position to coach these very teachers; finding that far too many go home exhausted, defeated, and ineffective. If this sounds familiar, take a deep breath and let it out. There's hope! The maneuvers presented in this book will help you take command of

Contents

GUERRILLA WARFARE TEACHING MANEUVERS

The Pocket Guide

Take Back Your Power Using Five Proven Teaching Grenade Tactics

MILTON LEE

PETERS

your classroom and allow you to leave at the end of your workday, empowered, energized, and successful. I want to give you five proven guerrilla warfare teaching maneuvers that will change your classroom and your life within 10 days.

Before we get into maneuvers, recognize that the environment in your classroom starts and ends with you. Know that you establish the atmosphere by your mood and your demeanor. Keep calm at all times and avoid becoming overly emotional with joy or anger. Students, much like a herd of wild animals, can sense even the slightest emotional instability. Expect to be observed and analyzed as they sniff for imbalance to green-light their attack. Develop and practice an unwavering professional determination. Whether you've had a terrible day or an amazing one, the class should never be the wiser. An even temperament is the first step towards stability. Remain cognizant that some students lack structure at home; routines and attitudes may be unpredictable, creating anxiety. When they enter your class, structure and emotional stability is what they need most. Give it to them. The success of every maneuver I share with you depends on it.

GUERRILLA WARFARE TEACHING MANEUVER #1
OPTIMIZE YOUR TERRAIN

Strategic Seating

Hands down, strategic seating is the maneuver with the most rapid and powerful result. Careful attention to your arrangement is crucial to optimizing the terrain. This maneuver instantly reminds students that you are in control. When a class is in a state of disorder, this will fast-track classroom management.

Aim for proximity to as many students as possible with as few steps as possible. Separate or add space between desks if cooperative groupings become problematic. Consider a variety of arrangements until you find one that works. The examples on the next page are some that I recommend.

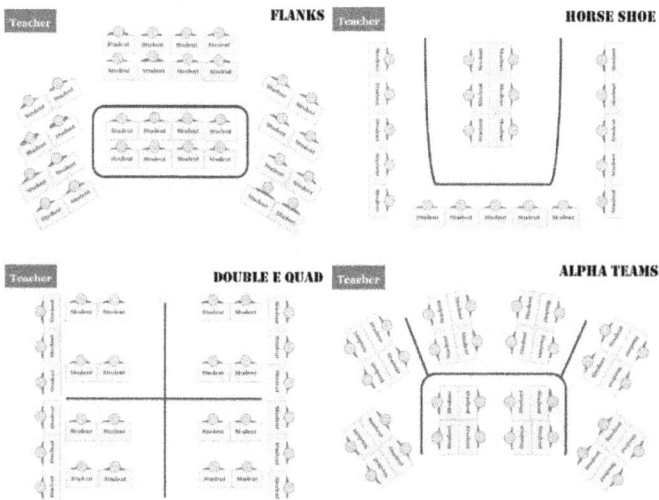

The solid lines in the diagrams represent the teacher walking path of maximum proximity; i.e., the interior loop. While this pathway should be your general moving area, don't rely solely on this route. Be everywhere.

Calculated Moves

Though it may be misunderstood, seat assignment is critical. When performed correctly, it will change the dynamics in an undisciplined class. Determine early on which personalities make a good match. At the beginning of the school year, this process is a guessing game that you will need to refine. Take time to identify behaviors and personality types. Then you'll be in a position to execute precise, calculated maneuvers.

Plan your line of attack. Sitting two socialites next to one another is asking for problems. Sitting a socialite beside an introvert is a much better match. Grouping all your loud mouth disruptors at the same table may not be the best move. Seating a loud mouth disruptor at a table of high achievers may be a better choice. Placing a meticulous pupil next to a pupil who is decidedly not, is another interesting combination. Think carefully about who will be close to the door, and the back or front of the room. Be prepared to change placements that aren't producing the desired result after a week. Remember these are carefully planned, strategic moves to achieve an expected reaction or outcome.

A scientific approach will be most effective, and quite possibly entertaining. Jot down observation notes to assess progress. Print or draw your chart, insert names, and project it from your document camera or computer. When students enter your class and see their name and seat, teach them to make a seamless adjustment. Allow no dissention or public protest. Explain early on that seating in your class is at your sole discretion, and subject to continual modification.

Stay Mobile

Know that in any seating arrangement you decide on, proximity is key. Invest in some comfortable combat boots and start marching. When students look left, be on their right. As they look right, pop-up on their left. When they peer ahead, materialize behind them. Your students should be keenly aware, that like the Almighty, you are everywhere, watching. Staying mobile throughout the lesson will discourage mounting insurrections.

Minimize your time at the whiteboard. Current technology makes this less of an issue than it once was. If you must work from the board, visually scan the class in a side stance as you're writing. Do not turn your back to the class. Try selecting a few scholars with good penmanship to go to the whiteboard and write important points from your notes while you maintain proximity with the class. If students frequently work on laptops or Chromebooks, an arrangement that will allow a full view of laptop screens, from one location, is essential. Unless of course, the school you are working at has taken steps to support teachers with monitoring software like GoGuardian, LightSpeed, and Netop Vision.

GUERRILLA WARFARE TEACHING MANEUVER #2

LOGISTICS

Simple Procedures

Logistics refers to, "the handling of the details of an operation" or procedures. Start teaching this from the moment you begin taking control of your classroom. The goal is, from the time students walk through your door until the time the bell rings, they know and operate within your procedural guidelines. Make expectations simple and clear. If a student does not know what they should do, they will inevitably do what they know they should not.

How students enter your class sets the tone for the lesson. When students arrive, they will adapt to the atmosphere you create. Have a procedure for it. For example:

Procedures Upon Entering My Classroom:

- ➢ ENTER QUIETLY.
- ➢ SHARPEN YOUR PENCIL(S) AS SOON AS YOU ENTER OR USE MECHANICAL PENCILS.
- ➢ TAKE YOUR ASSIGNED SEAT.
- ➢ WORK QUIETLY ON THE DAILY WARM-UP.
- ➢ REMAIN QUIET. IF YOU FINISH EARLY, CHECK THE WHITEBOARD FOR INSTRUCTIONS.

Practice Makes Perfect

Practice the direction you give for entering. Non-compliance must be quickly addressed. Don't hesitate to direct students to exit your room and come back in again. Prepare for students to test your commitment. Be consistent and stay calm. Understand that if you cave on one procedure you enact, you cave on them all. There may be occasions when the entire class needs to exit and re-enter correctly. Do this as many times as it takes to get it right. With difficult cases, I've seen this process take up to 20 minutes of instructional time. Stick with it. The payoff will be worth it. Don't allow students to put their backpacks or their supplies in your room until they enter correctly. Once students understand that you are unwavering and stable, they will conform. Remember that instruction cannot begin until you've established an environment conducive to learning.

Define logistics for all your routine and daily tasks. Have a procedure for passing paper. For example, if your students are in rows, you may direct them to pass papers to the left. Students on the farthest (last left column) are to pass papers forward. The person closest to the student bins should place work accordingly. Or, if students are in groups, have them stack papers in a certain manner within the group and have 1-2 people collect. Conduct timed drills to practice this procedure. Let them know you're serious about lost instructional minutes while creating an element of competition; as they work to improve on their last recorded time. Aim for under two minutes for the entire collection process. Providing a plan like this prevents students from roaming around the room. It also prevents distractions and off task behavior, which takes even more time to correct. Systematically rehearsing a paper collection procedure can prevent untold chaos.

Have a procedure for students speaking and getting your attention. Be extremely specific. Have a procedure for make-up and late work. Students should not interrupt your instruction to ask, "What did I miss...?" Have a procedure for exams, attendance, lineup, school site drills, etc. Eight to ten is a doable number to start with. Cover the main tasks to establish and keep classroom order without making the list overwhelming. Ensure these procedures are kept in students' binders. Have them enlarged and posted in your room. Send them home to be read and signed by a parent or guardian. Make sure to get the bottom signature portion returned to you. Then practice, drill, and rehearse until your classroom runs like a well-oiled machine. No matter how wonderful your lesson plan is, you will not adequately teach it if you have not taught logistics first.

GUERRILLA WARFARE TEACHING MANEUVER #3

SUPREME GOVERNANCE

Limit your Speech

Supreme governance means consistent exercise of your authority without argument. Your class rules and system of governance are non-negotiable. Enforce a program that includes simple rules, rewards, and discipline (emphasis on simple). Include them in your syllabus. Post your rules. Number them so that when you observe one being broken, you can state the rule number. "Marlene, Rule #3" is an example of a warning. Limit your speech as much as possible in these moments. Use nonverbal gestures such as, tapping on a desk as you walk by an off-task student. Don't let the warning detract from your instruction. Give as little attention to it as you can without ever ignoring it. Speaking too much to a student who is breaking the rules does two things. First, it offers the unruly student a sympathetic audience, and this may be what they want. Second, it takes away from the productive learning environment you've established. Like a soap opera, students will become more interested in the mounting conflict between you and the rule-breaker… while interest in your lesson disintegrates. Don't allow this to happen.

Warm Accolades and TEA

Rewards are wonderful and we all enjoy receiving them. But remember, the most meaningful reward is a feeling of self-worth and achievement. Yes, I know this sounds corny; Nevertheless, it's true. Whenever you determine a verbal accolade is warranted, give it. For example, "Class today you performed the paper passing procedure with flawless precision; Great job." Be specific when you give verbal praise so students learn exactly what you saw and liked. Trust me, when you take the time to acknowledge good behavior; they will repeat that same behavior.

Another tried-and-true reward strategy is Time Earned Activity or TEA. This works especially well if you have student group work. Establishing a point system for good conduct that allows students to select an approved activity at the end of the week can be just the added motivation some kids need. Determine a point goal. When the target is met, invite them to TEA. Students who are not invited must continue with the regularly scheduled assignment. If you use this incentive, stress that TEA is a privilege not a right. It's earned, and once earned, will not be taken away. Provide pupils with a list of appropriate TEA ideas and allow them to choose from that list. Use any acronym for this you want; A time earned point system works regardless of what you name it.

Ed Code Briefing

Make sure your discipline policy is realistic. Include parent contact in your plan. Some parents will be your greatest ally. Reach out with positive comments not just concerns. Use referrals with caution, as a last resort. Reserve them for the defiant knuckleheads that seem hellbent on causing troublesome uprisings or belligerent outbursts. That said, no matter how much your administration may discourage them, you are endowed with the lawful authority to write them. After a certain number of them, administration is bound to take escalating action such as student suspension or expulsion. Know that you also have authority to suspend a student from your class. This seems to be a well-kept secret at some school sites. It is nevertheless a power the classroom teacher can and should exercise if a student is hostile or continually causing willful disruption to the learning environment.

During the class suspension, administration may assign the delinquent to a designated discipline room for the day of suspension and the following day, or they may sit in the office. The important thing is that you remove the offender and restore control. When a Campus Supervisor escorts an, obstinate, knucklehead up to the office with *your* suspension slip in hand, you have pounded the gavel and demonstrated your supreme governance. Launch this

Guerrilla Warfare grenade, and it will not be forgotten by the offender or wide-eyed onlookers.

In the State of California for example, Ed Code 48910, clearly explains the teacher's right to suspend:

EDC 48910.

> (a) <u>A teacher may suspend any pupil from class, for any of the acts enumerated in Section 48900, for the day of the suspension and the day following.</u> The teacher shall immediately report the suspension to the principal of the school and send the pupil to the principal or the designee of the principal for appropriate action. If that action requires the continued presence of the pupil at the school site, the pupil shall be under appropriate supervision, as defined in policies and related regulations adopted by the governing board of the school district. As soon as possible, the teacher shall ask the parent or guardian of the pupil to attend a parent-teacher conference regarding the suspension. If practicable, a school counselor or a school psychologist may attend the conference. A school administrator shall attend the conference if the

16

teacher or the parent or guardian so requests. <u>The pupil shall not be returned to the class from which he or she was suspended, during the period of the suspension, without the concurrence of the teacher of the class and the principal</u>

(c) A teacher may also refer a pupil, for any of the acts enumerated in Section 48900, to the principal or the designee of the principal for consideration of a suspension from the school.

Become familiar with Ed Code Law in the state you teach and share this with colleagues who may also be in the trenches. You are not powerless to stop daily assaults on your classroom learning environment. Knowledge is power. You can look-up the **School Discipline Laws & Regulations by State** with the following URL: <<u>https://safesupportivelearning.ed.gov/school-discipline-laws-regulations-state</u>>.

Reporting class suspension to the principal is easy. Your school site or district office will likely have a form for this. If they don't, you'll find an example in the back of this book. Keep hard copies and an electronic version.

GUERRILLA WARFARE TEACHING MANEUVER #4
KNOW THY ENEMY

Proceed with Caution

As you get to know the student personalities in your room, identify the ringleaders — quickly. They're often the mastermind behind every class uprising. If unchecked, they will attempt a hostile takeover and cause your hard work and composure to go up in smoke. Unlike the average defiant knucklehead, ringleaders are charming and possess power to influence large groups of people. This is why they must be handled carefully. If they sense they are losing ground, they may devise elaborate plans to sabotage, malign, or discredit you. It's imperative that you not only pinpoint these individuals but beat them at their own game.

Assign Leadership Roles

In the words of Sun Tzu, "Know thyself, know thy enemy." Understanding the mindset of a ringleader is the first step to converting an enemy to an ally. A popular tactic in the military is to give the rebellious recruits more responsibility and leadership opportunities. This same maneuver can be applied to students. The ringleader desires followers and an audience. So, willingly offer them. Do this, of course, under the umbrella of your authority. Never relinquish your command to a ringleader. They will lose all respect for you and dismiss you and your instructions accordingly.

Instead, give the ringleader opportunities to prove himself to you. This becomes an intriguing challenge that will keep him occupied with something other than his nefarious conquests. Decide how you will allow the ringleader to demonstrate his competence with specific tasks. Make the ringleader responsible for special errands; answer the phone, write your instructions on the board, lead in group discussions and assignments, or act as a facilitator during projects. Start small until some level of trust is established, then gradually increase his or her leadership role. Find ways to utilize the ringleader's unique skill set. In other words, find out what the ringleader is good at and maximize it to your advantage. With this covert maneuver, you will vanquish an adversary while winning support and influence.

GUERRILLA WARFARE TEACHING MANEUVER #5
GUERRILLA GAZE

Remote Control

In the introduction I explained that your classroom environment starts and ends with you. The success of each maneuver will depend on your internal stability, and sheer resolve. If you're a teacher who is severely downtrodden by a calamitous classroom you will simply need to fake-it-till-you-make-it. Hold your ground. Once you begin implementing Guerrilla Warfare Teaching Maneuvers, you'll start to see changes in your class; providing encouragement until you win the war.

Appearing to be at ease and in complete control is half the battle. It's time to discuss the power of a single look. Picture a gaze that not only looks at you, but into you. A confident, poised, and powerful inspection of your very soul. If you happened to be... in the midst of an unsavory act during this visual examination, it would most certainly cause you to stop and evaluate yourself. This... is the guerrilla gaze. Stand in front of a mirror and rehearse this look until it develops naturally. Your face and jaw should be relaxed, mouth closed but lips at ease. Your brow should be smooth; eyes fixed and penetrating. Practice breathing through the look, inhaling and exhaling effortlessly. When you have mastered it, you will be able to stop unproductive behavior from across the room without a single word or gesture. Your look indicates a commitment to follow through whenever a violation occurs.

Practical Application

Now, visualize a student covertly fashioning a paper projectile under his desk; fully intent on pitching it across the room in hopes of making contact with the back of someone's head. You of course, are patrolling the room, quickly notice this stealthy preparation, and deploy the guerrilla gaze. The prankster feels your laser-like focus on him, looks up apologetically, and places the balled-up paper on top of his desk. Mission aborted. No words are spoken, while the rest of the class works quietly, oblivious to the averted disruption.

This can also be applied to students who are openly defiant or confrontational. Picture a student who attempts to talk over you or blurt out nonsense. Pause and initiate the guerrilla gaze. The class turns to witness her reaction. The student becomes conscious that all eyes are on her, and not in a good way. Flushed and uncomfortable, she shrugs, looks down and begins working; self-correcting her behavior.

I first learned the power of a single look in my early years of teaching after reading the book, *Tools for Teaching*, by Fred Jones. In fact, a good deal of my management style was influenced by this author. He describes, among other things how body language, including a specific look, can stop off task behaviors. I can certainly testify to this. When this maneuver has been utilized, time after time, I have seen willful defiance morph into apologetic shame --within seconds.

GUERRILLA WARFARE TEACHING MANEUVERS

CONCLUSION

War and Peace

Many battles may be fought before ultimate victory is achieved. As you begin demonstrating your authority, you will face initial resistance. Press forward. You may need to make a public announcement to prepare your students for the change ahead. For example, "Class, I will be making changes over the next couple weeks to improve the learning environment." Provide no further explanation and don't allow time for questions. Take command and deploy your first maneuver with level-headed precision. From this point forward your actions will speak louder than your words.

Change is a process. If you have lost control of your class recognize that it will take some time to completely turn things around. But with these five maneuvers, you'll be on your way to seeing results within 10 days. Stick with it and you will win the war; experiencing the pleasure of a well-managed class.

You'll be able to enjoy teaching while your students enjoy undistracted learning. You have the power to create and maintain a classroom environment that is structured, effective, and peaceful.

EXAMPLE N.O.S.S.

FROM THE DESK OF (TEACHER NAME)

DATE: _____   TIME: _____

NOTIFICATION OF STUDENT SUSPENSION

Dear _____   of _____
NAME OF PRINCIPAL OR DESIGNEE   NAME OF SCHOOL

Under provisions of CA Education Code 48910 I am class suspending:

_____
STUDENT NAME

for the remainder of today _____ and for all of the next school day _____

I am sending this pupil to you for appropriate action. I will notify the pupil's parent or guardian that I am requesting a parent-teacher conference regarding this suspension. Upon this pupil's return, I shall determine whether tests or assignments missed due to the suspension need to be completed.

Sincerely, _____
TEACHER'S SIGNATURE

48900 ED CODE LETTER PROCEEDS VIOLATION CHECKED

_____ Disruptive behavior or willful defiance of valid authority (k)

_____ Obscenity, habitual vulgarity, profanity (i)

_____ Causing, attempting or threatening violence or physical injury (a)

_____ Damage to school property or personal property (f)

_____ Possessing or being under the influence of any controlled substance or paraphernalia (c)

This list is not exhaustive but covers top 5

Description of Incident: _____

_____

THANK YOU FOR READING. IF YOU LIKE GUERRILLA WARFARE TEACHING MANEUVERS, THE POCKET GUIDE, OR FOUND IT HELPFUL IN ANY WAY PLEASE LEAVE AN AMAZON REVIEW.

☆☆☆☆☆

www.ingramcontent.com/pod-product-compliance
Lightning Source LLC
Chambersburg PA
CBHW070804050426
42452CB00012B/2488